EPIPHANY!

Power Statements
That Change Your Life

EPIPHANY!

Power Statements
That Change Your Life

Chandra Alexander MSW

Coaching for Authenticity, Inc.

Published by
Coaching for Authenticity, Inc.
3211 W Swann Ave, #605
Tampa, FL 33609 USA

Published 2009

EAN-13: 978-0-9778408-3-0 (paperback)
EAN-13: 978-0-9778408-4-7 (e-book)

Library of Congress Control Number: 2009912989

Printed in the United States of America

This book is for every brave soul who has done the work, and stayed awake when it was easier to go to sleep. I dedicate this to you.

Introduction

Nothing is more uplifting than an epiphany! One minute you are just "you", seeing things the way you always see them, and the next instant you are catapulted into a new state of consciousness. In this ahhhaa moment, the veil is lifted and truth is revealed. An epiphany is that truth, but what we do with that moment of clarity is really what matters.

Having an epiphany is a state of grace. Regardless of what you believe, when the mind is quiet, the heart opens. In this open-hearted state, we are privy to all information, especially information that has our best interests at heart; and the universe delivers. Often we get an unexpected answer that demands we head in a new direction, sometimes we "see" things we wish we had not seen, but always we see to the core of how things really are. This is information that is meant precisely for us.

The great thing about epiphanies is that they are totally unsolicited; they come about when you least expect them. You are not on a quest, not searching tirelessly for answers, but merely minding your own business, not anticipating any change, and along comes a mind-blowing insight that has the potential to rock your world. What you do with that information is what creates your life!

Power statements bring epiphanies that have the ability to transform your consciousness. Taking complicated concepts and distilling them into a power punch of a few words, a power statement delivers a bolt that pierces the illusion and re-scrambles your brain; the old way of thinking is gone! Power statements automatically penetrate the layers of the waking state and allow you to access the inner sanctum. By bypassing the intellect, you automatically feel rather than think, and that feeling state opens you to a deeper place of knowledge and understanding.

Everyone can have an epiphany but not everyone can learn from one! Realizations that are not accompanied with action fall by the wayside. If you fail to act and ignore your epiphanies, they will stop coming. Like an atrophied muscle, intuition gets stronger and stronger the more you trust and the more you put those insights into action in your everyday life. Without action, realizations will never bear fruit.

These power statements are my gift to you. Although it seems like they come from me, they really come THROUGH me, the same way your epiphanies come to you – unexpected, unadorned, and crystal clear; a bright light in a sometimes dark world, and a new way of looking at the same old stuff.

Here's to insights that crack the illusion and set you free!!

~ Chandra

You are always in the right place at the right time.

What you are most afraid of sets you free.

We all have stuff and no one's stuff is any better or worse than anyone else's; it's just that mine is mine and yours is yours.

Anger is really sadness flipped upside down.

It is better to feel right than to be right.

The space between the
old way not working
and the new way
not yet found is where
consciousness expands;
stay in the gap!

CHANDRA ALEXANDER

The future is nothing more than your present projected forward.

When you know how to take care of yourself, you are not afraid to open to love.

We never get tired of being loved.

Feeling something is always better than feeling nothing.

Being authentic is a process that happens over a lifetime and simultaneously takes place in the moment.

Time is neutral and does nothing but pass; things that are good get better and things that are bad get worse.

The more we do something the more critical mass it gains and the faster it moves; in other words, it begins to have a life of its own.

When you are confused, do nothing.

Confusion points the way to a new beginning and will not allow us to take the first path that allays our anxiety.

*Every time you trust
your inner voice, your
intuition gets stronger.*

Fear is neither good nor bad; it is simply a barometer that tells us we are entering unknown territory.

Never allow fear to be an option for not doing the things you want.

CHANDRA ALEXANDER

What if feeling the fear was actually different than reacting to it?

It is only when we run that the "creepies" run after us.

CHANDRA ALEXANDER

Real bravery comes when we confront our fears: when we stay and look rather than run and hide.

There is no timetable for getting clear, only a commitment we make to be real, no matter how long that takes.

*It takes a while to turn
a jet plane around but
when it finally turns,
it is going in a new
direction.*

What often feels most comfortable is not always in our best interest, but merely the way we have always done it.

The instant you become open to the possibility that there may be another way of looking at the same old stuff, something shifts.

Authenticity requires fearfulness; you have to be willing to see things differently and then do it differently.

It takes tremendous bravery to look at a life that is full of human frailties as well as triumphs and accept it wholly as your own.

When you are disciplined enough to change what doesn't work, you instantly have self-respect and self esteem.

*Once you know your
own stuff, it's only stuff.*

It is not what happens to us in a life but how we deal with what happens to us.

Real change takes place one choice at a time. Change one thing!

Doing things differently requires discipline; insight alone is not enough.

CHANDRA ALEXANDER

Taking responsibility for your life means: if it happened to you it belongs to you.

*When you miss
the signs and signals,
the universe ups the ante.*

You are responsible for the ingredients, not the outcome.

When your life is too full, you run out of space to grow.

Partitioning a life is a game the mind plays; you have only one heart.

Reality is all of life, not just the parts you are good at.

A person who has inner authentic presence has worked on himself, stays on the path no matter what, and chooses *Truth* even when it is inconvenient or uncomfortable.

CHANDRA ALEXANDER

You cannot have a good life unless you are brave.

Learning to love isn't easy. You have to stay open when you want to close and you have to look in deep, dark places when it is easier not to.

Real loving does not happen inadvertently; we choose to love.

If you don't know and like yourself, as another person moves close to you, you will pull away; we will not let someone else see what we have not seen.

We do not want to be loved in spite of our humanity, but because of it.

Loving is an introspective process — only when you know and love yourself can you love another.

If you want love, you must be love.

CHANDRA ALEXANDER

When you can take care of yourself, only then, do you pull to you someone who can take care of you.

Contrary to popular belief, you can't work on a relationship. The only thing you can ever work on is yourself.

You have all the time in the world and not a moment to waste.

When you close one door, don't open another; stand there, another door will open.

CHANDRA ALEXANDER

The universe is abundant and generous; simply by being on this earth you are worthy of all life's bounty.

The space between what you think and how the universe truly unfolds determines the amount of incongruity in your life.

When our life flows it is because our opinion of how it works and the way it really works are the same.

When you are doing work you love and that work flows THROUGH you – you are doing your life's work.

It is only when we move from the known to the unknown that energy has a place to grow and expand and create new ways for us to express ourselves.

CHANDRA ALEXANDER

In learning how to create your world, it is important to elicit the help of someone who is clearer than you are.

CHANDRA ALEXANDER

When you are confused, there is an incongruity between what you are feeling and what you are thinking.

When all the energy is in your head, you end up listening to everyone else's voice other than your own.

In order to touch the essence of something, we must be willing to bypass the mind and rest in the heart.

When the mind is quiet, the heart opens.

Like a leopard's spots, to the mind, all thoughts are neutral and the same; it is only our internal judge that qualifies thoughts as good and bad, pure and impure.

CHANDRA ALEXANDER

"*Trying*" *to quiet the mind is like saying, "Don't think of a monkey.*"

CHANDRA ALEXANDER

Thinking keeps you in your head; feeling connects you to your heart.

You only have one heart; if you close it to hurt, you also close it to love.

If you don't like who you are, you will never allow anyone to get close to you.

When people have trouble holding their own – rather than rise to the occasion and become more – they often want you to become less.

How you treat someone else says more about you than it does about them.

Generosity of spirit
means you want the
same good things for
others that you want
for yourself.

Ultimately, whom we love is less important than how we love.

You can't spoil someone with too much loving.

To know your Self is to know another, and there is nothing more tender than being known.

You cannot have compassion unless you have willingly felt your own fears and sorrows.

Real forgiveness occurs when you can be thankful for a painful experience, knowing it has added texture and substance to your life and made you what you are today.

CHANDRA ALEXANDER

Loving your Self is the same as taking care of yourself.

Nothing is more unattractive than whining and complaining.

What initially is uncomfortable ultimately nourishes our soul.

The "ugly cry" breaks up the barnacles on the heart.

Healing is a function of consciousness.

The universe works if you get out of the way.

No matter how much you study philosophy or practice spiritual disciplines, if it takes you away from your humanity, it is doing you a disservice.

You cannot exchange your assets for your liabilities.

*Without discipline,
nothing is possible.*

At every moment, we are living out our destiny and at that very same moment, with our free will, we are creating a new destiny.

CHANDRA ALEXANDER

*If you try a new way,
you'll get a new result.*

Just because you have been with someone for a long time does not mean you have to stay forever.

The unknown is scary, but not as scary as becoming less to stay.

In relationships with no promise of growth or change, eventually we leave – or worse, we stay.

Unless you have a true heart connection, longevity is never a reason for staying together.

---

*Chemistry keeps us
from paying attention
to the red flags only to
discover the red flags
get stronger.*

We are hard-wired for chemistry; it is in our make-up, in our genetic structuring.

It is only when you can take care of yourself that you can choose freely.

As long as you
rationalize an
undesirable situation
so you can stay, you
will never do what
you need to do to leave.

We all want so much for love to succeed that we feel like a failure even when we want to go.

When people are not meant to be together anymore, they're not.

We cry for the dreams
(not reality) that don't
come true.

In all strong, healthy relationships, people have fun.

Real sexuality is not about sex.

Rather than visualize the man of your dreams, feel what that feels like.

Knowing what you need always buys you more than money could buy.

What is good usually feels good.

What you are seeking is also seeking you.

Trusting the bullshit meter always gives us the edge.

Living in your head always keeps you one step away from the action.

EPIPHANY! Power Statements That Change Your Life

Paying attention to your feelings keeps you connected to your soul's work.

When we take a job we don't really want with the hope of it being a stepping stone to a job we covet, we will not like going to work every day.

What is a priority at one time in your life is not necessarily a priority at another.

Sometimes our most profound lessons come from brief interludes; just long enough to change a life forever.

Nothing is more loving than paying attention.

To really know something, you have to experience it unconditionally.

A still mind is the bedrock of creation.

True elegance is not possible unless it is connected to the Self.

"Getting it" means getting out of your own way.

The universe operates with speed and efficiency in direct relation to our degree of trust.

Nothing is more potent than sixth sense information.

There is a way the universe unfolds whether you get it or not.

A busy life is not the same as a life of substance.

Constant re-hashing
keeps you stuck!

Agendas push people away.

If you're bored with your story, it's time to change.

The more we delight in our own quirkiness, the more the world becomes a fun place to be.

Love grows if you're not in a coma.

The inner voice not only tells us once what we need to know, it nags us.

All illness, regardless of what it is, is a cry for consciousness.

ALL of your life belongs to you; you do not get to feel proprietary only when it suits you or things are going your way.

*When family members
are judged as friends,
then we've finally got it.*

Workaholics miss all the action.

Just like rings, bracelets, earrings and necklaces are made from the same block of gold; likewise we are consciousness that has been encapsulated in human form.

CHANDRA ALEXANDER

Peace is the result of clarity, a rock solid feeling that is stark and without embellishment of any kind.

Real bravery comes when we confront our fears: when we stay and look rather than run and hide.

A present life is the opposite of a conditional one.

What you set up at the beginning is what you have at the end.

For the last seven years, I have started each day by sending out a "wake-up" daily email to thousands of subscribers. The list has grown over the years and all your positive feedback inspired this book:

"Chandra is Tampa's very own 'Dr. Phil.' Straightforward, to the point and doesn't fool around. When it comes to a 'Reality Check' she doesn't pull any punches. We love her weekly segment and so do our viewers." April K. Wilson, Senior Producer, NBC/DAYTIME

"I have never seen anyone understand romantic relationships as deeply, clearly, and thoroughly as you. The way you cut through all the complicated dysfunctional behavior and expose relationships for, quite simply, what they really are, and what sabotages them, is amazing." - Debbie

"Just a quick note to tell you how just watching you on TV for the few minutes you were being interviewed has impacted my life in such a positive manner! Thank you for the words that jumped off the set and into my heart. I am so grateful for the words 'you must feel to heal' and I use this reminder multiple times, daily. Thank you. Thank you for giving me peace of mind and for helping my eyes focus on the future, instead of the rear view mirror." Kelly in Tampa

"Because I watched U from Palm Harbor between '02 and '06, I feel I have watched you evolve. Congrats! You are a lasting presence and I'm sure someone will be raised by the GIFT of your work!" Joie (now in St. Louis)

"Thank you again Chandra! If I may say so you are damn good at what you do and wonderful company!" Sincerely, Pam

"Just wanted to let you know that I had a major shift in my energy yesterday. The whole respect & self-respect thing was very powerful for me. I feel very solid today. Thank you for your generosity." Josie

"Our office now functions with extreme efficiency and productivity, very high moral, very low drama, and outstanding team spirit. None of the other consultants had been able to achieve the results we have seen since we employed Chandra. I cannot sing Chandra's praises loudly enough. If you are open to her insight, she will bring it with strength, confidence, and accuracy." Dawn R. Bhasin, M.D., Ophthalmologist and Oculoplastic Surgeon, VP, Guggino Family Eye Center

"Chandra! Don't want to think about where I would be without you. Thank you for holding my hand on my journey." Love, Hillary

"Over the past 18 months, my business has grown at a pace that I would have never expected and the main component of my success has come from Chandra's coaching. I feel that the time spent with her has been one of the best investments that I have ever made. Today, I have much better control and command over my personal and professional life." Jay S. Annis, CFP, CIMA Investment Consultant

"Chandra's unique approach gained immediate acceptance, approval and cooperation. Since we have adopted her directives, and recommendations, both administration and staff have been functioning and communicating at a significantly higher level." G.S. Guggino, M.D., F.A.C.S. CEO

"Hello Chandra, I have been a fan of yours for some time, receiving daily emails, reading your blogs and watching you on DAYTIME. I appreciate the fact that you focus forward and not backward." Michele

"Just wanted to say how much I admire you and everything you stand for. You are a great motivator. It is truely great to see authentic role models out there." Jacqueline

"i want to be you when i grow up. i'm 45 divorced and want to get it right this time!!!" Yours in health, Brenda

www.ingramcontent.com/pod-product-compliance
Lightning Source LLC
Chambersburg PA
CBHW072153270326
41930CB00011B/2411